WHO KILLED JESUS?

The Answer May Surprise You

Judy Kemp

Library of Congress Cataloging-in-Publication Data

Kemp, Judith (Judy)

Who Killed Jesus? The Answer May Surprise You

Includes bibliographical references

ISBN 978-1508411239 (softcover)

1. Death of Jesus – Easter – Lent – Christianity. I. Title
2015

Cover design: Editora Folego, Sao Paulo, Brazil and James Jacobson, the author's grandson

EXAMINING THE EVIDENCE

Preface

As you read the title of this book, you were probably thinking, "Where has she been all these years? Hasn't she seen the movies about Jesus? Hasn't she read the latest books about his death?

Yes, I have cried with you through the movies. Yes, I have been impressed with the historical details that the books' authors have added to my understanding.

However, there are some important questions that remain unanswered. Why did Jesus have to die? Who is ultimately responsible for his death?

Throughout history some have been assigned blame and have suffered because of it. I want you to know that it is not my desire to open old wounds. In fact, I think that the answer to these questions could bring relief and release from guilt to all.

I am a homemaker. I am not a theologian or a historian. I have, however, discovered the answer in the Holy Bible, the oldest and most reliable of all history books. I have read the accounts of the eyewitnesses. They have told me what they heard from Jesus' own mouth.

I hope that you will be enlightened by reading them too.

Chapter 1

Was it the religious leaders?

The first to know

The religious leaders of Jesus' day were some of the first to know of his birth. When the Magi arrived from the East after following the star, they asked King Herod, *"Where is he who has been born king of the Jews?"*

Herod was disturbed by the news of a possible rival and sought the help of the chief priests and teachers of the law to find him. He asked them where the Christ was to be born (Matthew 2:1-4).

They replied that it would be in Bethlehem, in the land of Judah and cited the prophecy from the Old Testament book of Micah: *"But you, O Bethlehem Ephrathah, who are too little to be among the clans of Judah, from you shall come forth for me one who is to be ruler in Israel, whose coming forth is from of old, from ancient days"* (5:2 – English Standard Version).

So, why didn't they go with the wise men to investigate? Were they the least bit concerned that the baby Herod said he wanted to worship (but later tried to kill), might possibly be the one they had been looking for?

The Jewish people at that time were under Roman rule. What they most dreamed of was having their Messiah arrive to restore their kingdom. They probably never imagined that he would come as a tiny, defenseless baby, but they should have, because that was prophesied too (see Isaiah 7:14 and 9:6).

They were not even curious enough to go see for themselves. They were just so busy with the "business" of religion that they had no time for the "essence" of it.

The first to criticize

Later, when he grew and began his ministry, Jesus just didn't fit within the parameters of the religious teaching of the day. He touched lepers. He ate with publicans and sinners. He talked with women as if they were equal with men. He healed on the Sabbath. His disciples didn't fast or wash their hands before eating.

These leaders tried to trick him with their questions. They watched as the respect, honor, and authority that they has received before, and felt they deserved, was turned onto Jesus.

The first to be criticized

Jesus always had time for the sick, the sinners, and the sincere seekers. But he had little patience with hypocrites and most of his harshest words were for the religious leaders of his day. He called them *"blind guides"*, *"blind fools"*, *"whitewashed tombs"*, *"serpents"*, *and a brood of vipers"* (Matthew 23:16, 17, 27, 33).

He accused them of doing their righteous acts to be

seen of men – announcing with trumpets their gifts to the needy, praying out loud on the street corners, disfiguring their faces so everyone would know that they were fasting (Matthew 6:1, 2, 5, 16). He accused them of nullifying the word of God for the sake of their traditions, and of teaching just rules taught by men. He said they worshipped God with their lips, but their hearts were far from him (Matthew 15:6-9). He told others not to follow their example, because they didn't practice what they preached. He accused them of tying heavy loads on others that they themselves couldn't bear. He even went to far as to say that they were shutting the kingdom of heaven in men's faces (Matthew 23:3, 13).

The first to want him dead

Is it any wonder that they wanted to get rid of this man? He was definitely bad for business! That's why they met in the palace of the high priest, Caiaphas, and plotted to arrest him (Matthew 26:3-4). They found him guilty in their own trial and handed him over to Pilate to be tried. During that trial, even Pilate recognized that it was out of envy that the religious leaders had handed Jesus over to him.

Yes, they wanted to kill him in the worst way. But were they responsible for his death?

Chapter 2

Was it Judas?

The chosen one

Jesus called twelve disciples to be with him. There was Simon (later called Peter and sometimes also known as Cephas) and his brother, Andrew. They were fishermen. James and his brother, John, sons of Zebedee, also fished for a living. For some reason they were called "the sons of thunder". The others were Philip, Bartholomew, Matthew (a tax collector, also called Levi), Thomas, another James (this one the son of Alphaeus), and Thaddaeus. Then, there was another Simon (known as the zealot), and, last of all, *Judas Iscariot, who betrayed him* (Mark 3:19). The account in Luke says, *...and Judas Iscariot, who became a traitor* (6:16).

At one point, Jesus said, *"Did I not choose you, the Twelve. And yet one of you is a devil"* (John 6:70).

The question that really needs to be answered is why did Jesus choose Judas?

This man was with the twelve from the beginning. He saw Jesus' power over sickness and disease when he healed the blind, the lame, the paralytics, and the lepers. He saw Jesus' power over death when he raised the widow's son, Jairus' daughter, and Lazarus. He saw the control that Jesus had over demons when he cast them out. He also knew that Jesus had control over nature when he calmed the sea with a word, walked on water, turned water into wine, and multiplied a little boy's lunch to feed a multitude with 5,000 families. Judas heard all Jesus' teachings and warnings. How, then, could he betray him?

The greedy one

Six days before Jesus' arrest, he was anointed by

Mary, Lazarus' sister. She took about a pint of pure nard, an expensive perfume, poured it on Jesus' feet and wiped his feet with her hair. However, we read: *But Judas Iscariot, one of his disciples (he who was about to betray him), said, "Why was this ointment not sold for three hundred denarii* (equal to a year's wages) *and given to the poor?" He said this, not because he cared about the poor, but because he was a thief, and having charge of the moneybag he used to help himself to what was put into it* (John 12:4-6).

I wonder how Judas came to be chosen treasurer for the group. We see from this story that he was a greedy, dishonest man. Did he betray Jesus just because of the money?

The indicated one

At the last supper, Jesus was troubled in his heart and finally said, *"Truly, truly, I say to you, one of you will betray me." The disciples looked at one another, uncertain of whom he spoke. One of his disciples, whom Jesus loved, was reclining at the table at Jesus' side, so Simon Peter motioned to him to ask Jesus of whom he was speaking. So that disciple, leaning back against Jesus, said to him, "Lord, who is it?"* (John 13:21-25).

In his gospel, Mark adds that when the disciples heard Jesus' words of his betrayal, *they began to be sorrowful and to say to him one after another, "Is it I?"* He said, *"I am not speaking to all of you; I know whom I have chosen. But the Scripture will be fulfilled, 'He who ate my bread has lifted his heel against me.'"* (John 13:8 – This prophecy is from Psalm 41:9). Then Jesus told them, *"It is he to whom I will give this morsel of bread when I have dipped it." So when he had dipped the morsel, he gave it to Judas* (John 13:26).

Judas replied, *"Surely not I, Rabbi?"* and Jesus answered, *"Yes, it is you"* (Matthew 26:25, NIV).

We read on John 13:27-30 that as soon as Judas took the bread from Jesus' hand, Satan entered into him. Jesus told him, *"What you are about to do, do quickly."* Apparently the other disciples didn't really understand why he had said this. They thought it might be because Jesus was telling him to get something that was needed for the feast, or to buy something for the poor, since he was the treasurer of the group.

In Matthew 26:24 Jesus added, *"The Son of Man goes as it is written of him, but woe to that man by whom the Son of Man is betrayed! It would have been better for that man if he had not been born."*

The one who betrayed Jesus

Actually, Judas was such a hypocrite when he asked Jesus, "Surely not I, Rabbi?" It appears that he had already betrayed Jesus before the Last Supper. In the Matthew account we read: *Then one of the twelve, whose name was Judas Iscariot, went to the chief priests and said, "What will you give me if I deliver him over to you?" And they paid him thirty pieces of silver. And from that moment he sought an opportunity to betray him (26:14-16).*

I guess it's possible that Judas was so greedy that he would betray his Rabbi for the money. Or maybe he saw that being one of Jesus' disciples wasn't as good of a deal as he had originally thought it would be. Perhaps he had hoped that Jesus would restore the kingdom and that, as a disciple, he would reign with him. Being chosen by Jesus didn't have quite the prestige and honor he had thought it would. He had probably heard rumors that the religious rulers wanted to imprison Jesus and might have been afraid that he also would be arrested because of his identification with the accused.

Judas had arranged a signal with those who paid him the money to betray Jesus, *"The one I will kiss is the man; seize him"* (Matthew 26:48). In the garden he went at once to Jesus and said, *"Greetings, Rabbi!"* and kissed him. Jesus asked, *"Judas, would you betray the Son of Man with a kiss?"* (Luke 22:48), and added, *"Friend, do what you came to do"* (Matthew 26:50).

The remorseful one

Early the next morning, all the chief priests and elders decided to put Jesus to death and handed him over to Pilate, the governor.

When Judas saw that Jesus was condemned, he was seized with remorse and returned the thirty silver coins to the chief priests and the elders. *"I have sinned,"* he said, *"for I have betrayed innocent blood."*

"What is that to us? That's your responsibility," they answered. So Judas threw the money at them and left the temple. Then he went out and hanged himself (Matthew 27:1-5).

Those leaders didn't know what to do with the money Judas had thrown at them, because it was blood money, and finally decided to use it to buy the potter's field as a burial place for foreigners. This fulfilled another Old Testament prophecy. In Zechariah 11:12-13 we read: *Then I said to them, "If it seems good to you, give me my wages; but if not, keep them." And they weighed out as my wages thirty pieces of silver. Then the LORD said to me, "Throw it to the potter" – the lordly price at which I was priced by them. So I took the thirty pieces of silver and threw them into the house of the LORD to the potter.*

Judas was filled with remorse, but was it true repentance? I think not. He was willing to admit that Jesus was an innocent man, but he still wasn't willing to believe that Jesus was who he said he was and had come to do what he said he was going to do. Because of this, he felt the situation was hopeless and saw no alternative but to take his own life.

The lost one

In his prayer recorded in John 17, Jesus refers to Judas as *"the one doomed to destruction"* (v.12, NIV). Jesus had told Judas that it would have been better that he had never been born.

Yes, he was eternally lost, but was he the one responsible for Jesus' death?

Chapter 3

Was it the false witnesses?

Those who had arrested Jesus took him to Caiaphas, the high priest, where the teachers of the law and the elders had assembled. This religious court was known as the Sanhedrin. We are told that the chief priests and the whole Sanhedrin were looking for false evidence against Jesus so that they could put him to death. But they did not find any, though many false witnesses came forward (Matthew 26:57-60). Finally, two declared:

"He said he was going to destroy God's temple"

More than once Jesus had prophesied that the temple would be destroyed. One of those times was right after he threw the money-changers out of God's house.

They demanded a miraculous sign to prove that he had authority to do everything that he was doing (including clearing out the temple).

Jesus answered them, "Destroy this temple, and in three days I will raise it up." The Jews wanted to know how he thought he could raise up the temple in three days when it had taken forty-six years to build. Then the Scripture adds: *But he was speaking about the temple of his body. When therefore he was raised from the dead, his disciples remembered that he had said this, and they believed the Scripture and the word that Jesus had spoken* (John 2:19-22).

When the false witness accused Jesus of this, the high priest asked him, "Aren't you going to defend yourself?" But Jesus remained silent.

"He is guilty of blasphemy!"

Next, the high priest said to Jesus, *"I charge you*

under oath by the living God: Tell us if you are the Christ, the Son of God."

And Jesus replied, *"Yes, it is as you say. But I say to all of you: In the future you will see the Son of Man sitting at the right hand of the Mighty One and coming on the clouds of heaven."*

Then the high priest tore his clothes and said, *"He has spoken blasphemy. Why do we need any more witnesses? Look, now you have heard the blasphemy. What do you think?"* They answered, *"He is worthy of death."* Then they spit in his face and hit him with their fists or slapped him. Some of them said, *"Prophesy to us, Christ. Who hit you?"* (Matthew 26:63-67, NIV).

To their way of thinking, anyone saying that he was equal with God was, of course, guilty of blasphemy. The Jews would continually repeat the phrase, "The LORD our God is one". One of the distinguishing factors of their religion, ever since its inception, was that it was monotheistic, in contrast to the other nations that were polytheistic.

The idea that God had a Son was new to them, but it shouldn't have been. When God created the earth, he said, *"Let US make man in our own image"* (Genesis 1:26 – emphasis mine). The Spirit of God moved upon the face of the waters (Genesis 1:2).

Psalm 2:12, a verse they had probably read often, said: *Kiss the Son, lest he be angry and you perish in the way.*

In Proverbs 30:4-5 (Proverbs is the Old Testament book of wisdom written by King Solomon), we read: *Who has ascended to heaven and come down? Who has gathered up the wind in his fists? Who has wrapped up the waters in a garment? Who has established all the end of the earth? What is his name, and what is his son's name? Surely you know?*

The Trinity is clearly revealed in the Old Testament as well as the new.

After Jesus healed the man who had been an invalid for thirty-eight years, the Jewish leaders criticized him for doing it on the Sabbath. Jesus told them, *"My Father is working until now, and I am working."* This same passage tells us that after this incident the Jews tried even harder to kill him, not just because he was breaking the Sabbath, but because he called God his own Father, making himself equal with God (John 5:16-18).

At the end of this same chapter, Jesus shows the Jews how they can know that he is the Son of God. He tells them to look at the testimonies:

His own testimony: Jesus said, *If I testify about myself, my testimony is not valid"* (John 5:31).

Obviously anyone can claim that he is God's Son. That's not enough. Many people believe that Jesus was a wonderful teacher and a great example for us to follow, but they don't believe that he is the Son of God. However, if Jesus was not God's Son, he was not a wonderful teacher or a great example. He was either a liar or crazy. As C.S. Lewis says, "Anyone who says he is the Son of God, when he is not, is equal to someone who claims he's a hard-boiled egg."[1]

What did Jesus say about himself?

"I am the Messiah" (John 4:25-26).

"I am the bread of life; whoever comes to me shall not hunger, and whoever believes in me shall never thirst (John 6:35).

"I am the light of the world. Whoever follows me will not walk in darkness but sill have the light of life" (John 8:12).

"I and the Father are one" (John 10:30).

"I am the good shepherd. The good shepherd lays down his life for the sheep" (John 10:11).

"I am the resurrection and the life. Whoever believes in me, though he die, yet shall he live, and everyone who lives and believes I me shall never die. Do you believe this?" (John 11:25-26).

"I am the way, and the truth, and the life. No one comes to the Father except through me" (John 14:6).

The human testimony: Jesus said, *"You sent to John and he has borne witness to the truth. Not that the testimony that I receive is from man, but I say these things so that you may be saved* (John 5:33-34).

Human beings can be easily deceived. It wouldn't have been the first time that someone had believed a lie. But what did those who knew Jesus best reveal about him?

His mother: "The angel told me, '...*behold, you will conceive in your womb and bear a son, and you shall call his name Jesus. He will be great and will be called the Son of the Most High*'" (Luke 1:31-32).

The disciples: When Jesus asked Peter, "Who do you say that I am?" he answered, *"You are the Christ, the Son of the living God"* (Matthew 16:15-16). John said, *"I have seen and I testify that this is the Son of God"* John 1:34, NIV). After Jesus walked on water to them, those disciples who were in the boat said, *"Truly you are the Son of God"* (Matthew 14:33). All of the eleven disciples, with the exception of John, were martyred because of their belief and their teaching that Jesus is the Son of God. Would they have died for a lie?

The Roman Guard: When the centurion, who was there at the crucifixion, saw how Jesus died, he said, *"Truly this man was the Son of God!"* (Mark 15:39).

God the Father's testimony: Jesus said, *"And the Father who sent me has himself borne witness about me* (John 5:35a).

God spoke from heaven and put his seal of approval

on his Son three times while Jesus was here on earth. One of those times was at Jesus' baptism when he said, *"You are my beloved Son; with you I am well pleased"* (Mark 1:11).

The second time was at Jesus' transfiguration. After seeing his Master talking with Moses and Elijah, Peter wanted to give each of them equal treatment and build three tents. That was only until he heard the voice of God coming from a cloud to tell him, *"This is my beloved Son, with whom I am well pleased; listen to him!"* (Matthew 17:5).

John records the third time in the twelfth chapter of his gospel. Jesus was in prayer before his crucifixion, and told his Father, *"Now my soul is troubled. And what shall I say? 'Father, save me from this hour'? But for this purpose I have come to this hour. Father, glorify your name." Then a voice came from heaven: "I have glorified it, and I will glorify it again."* Jesus told his disciples, *"This voice has come for your sake, not mine"* (verses 27-28,30).

The testimony of the miracles: Jesus said, *"I have a testimony weightier than that of John. For* *the very work that the Father has given me to finish, and which I am doing, testifies that the Father has sent me"* (John 5:36-NIV).

Because he said, "I and my Father are one," the Jews wanted to stone Jesus. So he asked them, *"I have shown you many great miracles from the Father. For which of these do you stone me?"*

"We are not stoning you for any of these," replied the Jews, *"but for blasphemy, because you, a mere man, claim to be God."*

"Why do you accuse me of blasphemy because I said, 'I am God's Son'? Do not believe me unless I do what my Father does. But if I do it, even though you do not believe me, believe the miracles, that you may know and understand that the Father is in me, and I in the Father" (John 10:30-33, 36b-38, NIV).

We have already seen Jesus' power over disease, death, demons, and nature. Have you studied the miracles he performed? What do they tell you about him?

In a sense, the miracles showed that what Jesus

said about himself was true. He said he was the bread of life and he fed a multitude of 5,000 families with a little boy's lunch. He said that he was the light of the world and he gave sight to a blind man. He said that he was the resurrection and the life and he raised people from the dead.

At the end of his gospel, John, the disciple of Jesus, wrote: *Jesus did many other miraculous signs in the presence of his disciples, which are not recorded in this book. But these are written that you may believe that Jesus is the Christ, the Son of God, and that by believing you may have life in his name* (John 20:30-31, NIV).

The testimony of Scripture: Jesus told his audience, *"You search the Scriptures because you think that in them you have eternal life; and it is they that bear witness about me, yet you refuse to come to me that you may have life"* (John 5:39-40).

Did Jesus fulfill the prophecies in the Old Testament about Messiah? We will look into this later, but let me assure you that he did.

But first, let's get back to the accusations of the false witnesses...

The religious leaders decided that Jesus was worthy of death because, according to them, he was guilty of blasphemy. There was a problem, however. They had to have an accusation that would stick with Pilate, the ruler of the Roman government in their area.

When they took Jesus to him, Pilate asked, *"What charges are you bringing against this man? "* to which they answered, *"If me were not a criminal, we would not have handed him over to you"* (John 18:29-30, NIV).

Now what kind of an accusation is that?

Pilate said to them, "Take him yourselves and judge him by your own law." The Jews said to him, "It is not lawful for us to put anyone to death." (John 18:31).

Since the Jews were under Roman rule, they really didn't have the right to execute anyone. That's why they had to go to a civil court and convince the Roman authorities that he was guilty of some crime that they would consider worthy of death. It wasn't easy. So, they tried saying, *"He is subverting the nation and stirring up a rebellion."*

"He is stirring up a rebellion"

When the chief priests and elders of the people came to arrest Jesus in the garden, he asked them, *"Am I leading a rebellion, that you have come out with swords and clubs to capture me? Every day I sat in the temple courts teaching and you did not arrest me. But this has all taken place that the writings of the prophets might be fulfilled"* (Matthew 26:55-56, NIV).

Pilate called together the chief priest, the rulers, and the people, and said to them, *"You brought me this man as one who was inciting the people to a rebellion. I have examined him in your presence and have found no basis for your charges against him"* (Luke 23:14, NIV).

"He opposes paying taxes to Caesar"

This was a bold-faced lie. In Matthew 22:15-22, NIV, the Pharisees went out and laid plans to trap

Jesus in his words. They sent people to ask, *"Teacher, tell us, what is your opinion? Is it right to pay taxes to Caesar or not?"*

Jesus answered, *"You hypocrites, why are you trying to trap me? Show me the coin used for paying the tax."* When they brought him a denarius, he asked, *"Whose portrait is this? And whose inscription?"*

"Caesar's," was their reply, to which Jesus answered, *"Give to Caesar what is Caesar's and to God what is God's."*

The Bible says that they were amazed when they heard this, left him, and went away.

"He claims to be king"

If they could make this accusation stick, there would be a good chance that Pilate would listen to them because he didn't want anyone else taking over his job or his kingdom.

Pilate asked Jesus, *"Are you the king of the Jews?"* Jesus replied, *"Yes, it is as you say"* (Mark 15:2).

"You are a king, then!" said Pilate.

Jesus answered, "You are right in saying I am king. In fact, for this reason I was born, and for this I came into the world, to testify to the truth (John 18:37, NIV).

He told Pilate, *"My kingdom is not of this world. If it were, my servants would fight to prevent my arrest by the Jews. But now my kingdom is from another place."*

Then Pilate announced to the chief priests and the crowd, *"I find no basis for a charge against him"* (John 18:36,38, NIV).

They must have been terribly disappointed with his response.

Were the false witnesses guilty of Jesus' death? How could they be if no one believed them?

The chief priests and the whole Sanhedrin were looking for evidence against Jesus so that they could put him to death, but they did not find any. Many testified falsely against him, but their statements did not agree (Mark 14:55-56, NIV).

These false witnesses didn't tell the truth about Jesus because they didn't know the truth about Jesus. That's why he said, *"Father, forgive them, for they know not what they do"* (Luke 23:34).

Chapter 4

Where were the witnesses for the defense?

There were many false witnesses at Jesus' trial, but where were the defense witnesses? Where were the people he had healed? Where were the multitudes he had fed? Where were the crowds who only a few days earlier had shouted, *"Hosanna to the Son of David! Blessed is he who comes in the name of the Lord! Hosanna in the highest!"* (Matthew 21:9).

Where were Jesus' disciples?

Toward the end of Jesus' ministry his disciples said, *"Now we know that you know all things and do not need anyone to question you; this is why we believe that you came from God.*

Jesus answered them, "Do you now believe? Behold, the hour is coming, indeed it has come, when you will be scattered, each to his own home, and will leave me all alone. Yet I am not alone, for the Father is with me" (John 16:30-32).

At the Last Supper, Jesus told them, *"You will all fall away because of me this night. For it is written, 'I will strike the shepherd, and the sheep of the flock will be scattered'"* (Matthew 26:31). This is another Old Testament prophecy that was fulfilled. It is from Zechariah 13:7.

Actually, Jesus' disciples were not present at the trial because he had sent them away. When the religious leaders came to arrest him in the garden, he said, *"...if you seek me, let these men go"* (John 18:8). Even in his hour of trial, when he so much needed support, the Good Shepherd thought only of his sheep.

"I will never fall away"

When Jesus said that the disciples would all fall away on account of him, Peter replied, "Though they all fall away because of you, I will never fall away."

Jesus said to him, "Truly, I tell you, this very night, before the rooster crows, you will deny me three times."

Peter said to him, "Even if I must die with you, I will not deny you!" And all the disciples said the same (Matthew 26:33-35).

Luke, in his account, added these words of Jesus, *"Simon, Simon, behold, Satan demanded to have you that he might sift you like wheat, but I have prayed for you that your faith may not fail. And when you have turned again, strengthen you brothers* (22:31).

"I will pray with him"

When Jesus was praying in the garden, he was in extreme anguish and sweat drops of blood. He told Peter, James, and John, *"My soul is very sorrowful, even to death. Remain here and watch* (Mark 14:34). He returned three times and each time found the disciples sleeping. He said to Peter,

"Simon, are you asleep? Could you not watch one hour? Watch and pray that you may not enter into temptation. The spirit indeed is willing, but the body is weak" (Mark 14:34, 37-38).

"I will fight for him"

Peter had the best of intentions. He really tried to be faithful and we have to give him credit for that. When Jesus was being arrested, we read: *Then Simon Peter, having a sword, drew it and struck the high priest's servant, and cut off his right ear. (The servant's name was Malchus.) So Jesus said to Peter, "Put your sword into its sheath; shall I not drink the cup that the Father has given me?"* (John 18:10-11)

"I never knew him"

As they led Jesus away from the garden to the house of the high priest, Peter followed at a distance (Luke 22:54). Someone had made a fire in the middle of the courtyard and he sat down with others who were trying to keep warm. A servant girl saw him, examined him closely, and said, *"This man was with him."* But he denied it. *"Woman, I don't know him."*

A little later someone else recognized him as one of Jesus' followers and he answered, *"Man, I am not."*

A third person confirmed about an hour later, *"Certainly this fellow was with him, for he too is a Galilean." But Peter said, "Man, I do not know what you are talking about"* (Luke 22:54-59).

Mark adds a bit more information that is not in Luke's account. When he was accused of being with Jesus, Peter began to call down curses on himself, and swore (14:71).

While he was still speaking, the rooster crowed. The Lord turned and looked at Peter and that's when he remembered what Jesus had said: *"Before the rooster crows today, you will deny me three times." And he went out and wept bitterly* (Luke 22:60-62).

I think I know how Peter must have felt when Jesus turned and looked straight at him. I have imagined that same look in Jesus' eyes myself when I have rebelled against him and gone my own way. In spite of our failings, it is always a look of love.

"I received a special invitation"

One wonders if Mark, when he wrote his gospel, didn't get a lot of information directly from Peter, because he has so many details that the others don't have. We know that after Jesus rose from the dead, the angel told the women at the tomb, *"Do not be alarmed. You seek Jesus of Nazareth, who was crucified. He has risen; he is not here. See the place where they laid him. But go, tell his disciples and Peter that he is going ahead of you into Galilee. There you will see him, just as he told you"* (Mark 16:6-7).

Go tell his disciples and Peter? But wasn't Peter a disciple? Why did he need a special invitation? It must have been because Jesus knew how deeply sorrowful and guilty Peter felt for having disowned him. If Jesus had only invited the disciples, Peter would probably have decided, "Certainly the Master doesn't want to see me after all I've done." But, then, the women would have told him, "No, Peter he DOES want to see you. He specifically mentioned your name!"

That's grace – and you can be sure that Peter understood it.

"I will feed his sheep"

The last verses of John's gospel record a conversation between Peter and Jesus after his resurrection. Three times Jesus asked this disciple, "Do you love me?" (Did he ask three times because Peter had denied him three times?)

When Peter answered each of the three times, *"Yes, Lord, you know that I love you,"* Jesus told him, *"Feed my lambs"* (John 21:15-17).

Yes, Peter would feed Jesus sheep. This time he kept his promise.

If you were going to start a new church, would you choose as the first pastor the man who had denied you three times? Jesus did. Peter understood grace, and what Jesus most wanted was a pastor who really understood grace. Who could possibly have understood it better than Peter?

What a powerful, fearless preacher he became!

At Pentecost Peter told the Jews, *"This Jesus God raised up, and of that we are all witnesses. Being therefore exalted at the right hand of God, and having received from the Father the promise of the Holy Spirit, he has poured out this that you yourselves are seeing and hearing*

Let all the house of Israel therefore know for certain that God has made both Lord and Christ, this Jesus whom you crucified."

So those who received his message were baptized, and there were added that day about three thousand souls (Acts 2:32, 36, 41).

"The God of Abraham, Isaac and Jacob, the God of our fathers, glorified his servant Jesus. You handed him over to be killed, and you disowned him before Pilate, though he had decided to let him go. You disowned the Holy and Righteous One and asked that a murderer be released to you. You killed the Author of life, but God raised him from the dead. We are witnesses of this.

Now, brothers, I know that you acted in ignorance, as did your leaders. But this is how God fulfilled what he had foretold through all the prophets, saying that his Christ would suffer. Repent, then, and turn to God, so that your sins may be wiped out, that times o refreshing may come from the Lord" (Acts 3:13-15, 17-19).

Peter knew that it was never too late to repent, no matter what the transgression. The book of Acts leaves it very clear that he suffered much persecution because of his identification with Christ, and yet he remained bold in his witness. History tells us that he was also crucified. Since he felt himself unworthy of dying as his Savior had, he asked to be crucified upside down.

If Jesus forgave Peter, and greatly used him, who am I to accuse him?

Chapter 5

Was it the political leaders?

As mentioned before, the Jews were under Roman rule and would have to convince the political authorities of Jesus' guilt if they were to succeed in getting him killed. They weren't having much success because:

Pilate wanted the Jews to try him according to their own law

When the religious leaders took Jesus to Pilate, he asked, *"What are the charges against him?"* and they answered, *"If he were not a criminal, we wouldn't have handed him over to you."* Pilate replied, *"Take him yourselves and judge him by your own law."* The Jews objected, *"But we have no right to execute anyone"* (John 18:29-31, NIV).

Pilate really wanted Jesus to defend himself

When he was accused by the chief priests and the elders, he gave no answer. Then Pilate asked, "Don't you hear the testimony they are bringing against you?" But Jesus made no reply, not even to a single charge – to the great amazement of the governor (Matthew 27:12-14, NIV).

Pilate said to them, *"Take him yourselves and crucify him, for I find no guilt in him." The Jews answered him, "We have a law, and according to that law he ought to die because he has made himself the Son of God." When Pilate heard this statement, he was even more afraid. He entered his headquarters again and said to Jesus, "Where are you from?" But Jesus gave him no answer. So Pilate said to him, "You will not speak to me? Do you not know that I have authority to release you and authority to crucify you? Jesus answered him, "You would have no authority over me at all unless it had been given to you from above. Therefore he who delivered me over to you has the greater sin* (John 19:6b-11).

Pilate wanted a confirmation from Herod

When Pilate heard that Jesus was a Galilean and under Herod's jurisdiction, he sent him to Herod, who was in Jerusalem at the time.

Herod had heard about Jesus and was glad to have an opportunity to see him. He hoped that maybe Jesus would perform another miracle or sign. However, Jesus gave no answer to his questions, while the chief priests and scribes stood by, vehemently accusing him. At Herod's direction, the soldiers treated Jesus with contempt, mocked him, and dressed him in some splendid clothing before sending him back to Pilate. The Scripture tells us that, although Herod and Pilate had always been enemies, that day they became friends (Luke 23:8-12).

When Pilate got the chief priest and the people together, he told them: *"You brought me this man as one who was misleading the people. And after examining him before you, behold, I did not find this man guilty of any of your charges against him. Neither did Herod, for he sent him back to us. Look, nothing deserving death has been done by*

49

him. I will therefore punish and release him" (Luke 23:13-16).

He wanted the religious leaders to convince him of Jesus' guilt

The Jews had a hard time coming up with an accusation that would stick. The first time Pilate asked them what charges they were bringing against Jesus, they answered, *"If he weren't guilty, we wouldn't have handed him over to you."* Pilate repeated the words, *"I found no basis for your charges against him"*, *"He has done nothing to deserve death"*, or *"What crime has he committed?"* at least five times during the trial.

He wanted to listen to his wife

While Pilate was sitting on the judge's seat, his wife sent him this message: "Don't have anything to do with that innocent man, for I have suffered a great deal today in a dream because of him" (Matthew 27:19, NIV).

He wanted to release Jesus and keep Barabbas

Barabbas had been thrown into prison for an insurrection in the city and for murder (Luke 23:19).

Now at the feast the governor was accustomed to release for the crowd any one prisoner whom they wanted. And they had then a notorious prisoner called Barabbas. So when they had gathered, Pilate said to them, "Whom do you want me to release for you: Barabbas, or Jesus who is called Christ?" For he knew that it was out of envy that they had delivered him up (Matthew 27:15-18).

Now the chief priests and the elders persuaded the crowd to ask for Barabbas and destroy Jesus. The governor again said to them, "Which of the two do you want me to release for you?" And they said, "Barabbas." Pilate said to them, "Then what shall I do with Jesus who is called Christ?" They all said, "Let him be crucified!" And he said, "Why, what evil has he done?" But they shouted all the more, "Let him be crucified!" (Matthew 27:20-23).

After that, Pilate still tried to release Jesus, but the Jews kept insisting, *"If you release this man, you are not Caesar's friend. Everyone who makes himself a king opposes Caesar."*

So, finally Pilate sat down on the judgment seat and had Jesus brought before him. *Now it was the day of Preparation of the Passover. It was about the sixth hour. He said to the Jews, "Behold your King!" They cried out, "Away with him, away with him, crucify him!" Pilate said to them, "Shall I crucify your King?" The chief priests answered, "We have no king but Caesar"* (John 19:12-15).

It seems that Pilate was starting to think that he would be in trouble with Caesar if he didn't give in to the wishes of the people.

He washed his hands of the whole deal

When Pilate saw that he was getting nowhere, but that instead an uproar was starting, he took water and washed his hands in front of the crowd. "I am innocent of this man's blood," he said. "It is your responsibility." All the people answered, "Let his blood be on us and on our children!" (Matthew 27:24-25, NIV).

Did Jesus hold Pilate responsible for his death? In John 19:11, he had told the governor, *"The one who handed me over to you is guilty of a greater sin."*

Pilate finally gave in to the pressure of the crowd

Wanting to satisfy the crowd, Pilate released Barabbas to them. He had Jesus flogged, and handed him over to be crucified (Mark 15:15).

So they took Jesus, and he went out, bearing his own cross, to the place called The Place of a Skull, which in Aramaic is called Golgotha. There they crucified him, and with him two others, one on either side and Jesus between them.

Pilate also wrote an inscription and put it on the cross. It read, "Jesus of Nazareth, the King of the Jews." Many of the Jews read this inscription, for the place where Jesus was crucified was near the city, and the sign was written in Aramaic, in Latin and in Greek. So the chief priests of the Jews said to Pilate, "Do not write 'The King of the Jews, but rather, 'This man said, I am King of the Jews.'" Pilate answered, "What I have written I have written" (John 19:17-22).

Actually, although Pilate didn't realize it, he was fulfilling Scripture. The prophecy of Jesus' death in Psalm 22 says *...they have pierced my hands and my feet* (verse 16b). At the time that this prophecy was written, hundreds of years before Jesus' birth, crucifixion was not used as a method of capital punishment. It was not until the Romans came into power that it was practiced.

Peter prayed to God in Acts 4:23-28. He said that Herod, Pontius Pilate, along with the Gentiles and the peoples of Israel gathered together *"...against your holy servant Jesus, whom you anointed ... to do whatever your hand and your plan had predestined to take place."*

Was this God's plan all along?

Chapter 6

Was it God the Father?

Jesus had told Pilate, "You would have no power if it were not given to you from above (John 19:11a, NIV). Did God the Father give Pilate the power to crucify His Son, Jesus?

When Peter cut off the ear of the priest's servant in the garden, Jesus told him, *"Put your sword away! Shall I not drink the cup the Father has given me?"* (John 18:11, NIV)

Jesus made it very clear that he had come to do the Father's will. He also made it very clear that it was God's will for him to give his life on the cross.

Just before his death, Jesus told his disciples, *"...the world must learn that I love the Father and that I do exactly what my Father has commanded me"* (John 14:31, NIV).

When he prayed in the garden, he told his Father *"...if it is not possible for this cup to be taken away unless I drink it, may your will be done"* John 26:42, NIV).

Jesus admitted, *"Now my heart is troubled and what shall I say? 'Father, save me from this hour?' No, it was or this very reason I came to this hour. Father glorify your name!"* (John 12:27-28, NIV)

He told his disciples, *"...the world must learn that I love the Father and that I do exactly what my Father has commanded me"* (John 14:31, NIV).

When the religious leaders came to arrest him, Jesus asked, *"Do you think I cannot call on my Father, and he will at once put at my disposal more that twelve legions of angels? But how then would the Scriptures be fulfilled that say it must happen this way?"* (Matthew 26:53, NIV)

Again, in Mark 14:21 Jesus told his disciples, *"For*

the Son of Man goes as it is written of him..."

What was written about him? One of the most descriptive prophesies in the Old Testament about the death of Christ is found in Isaiah chapter 53. This passage of Scripture makes it very clear who nailed Jesus to that cross.

Surely he took our infirmities and carried our sorrows, yet we considered him stricken by God, smitten by him, and afflicted. Yet it was the LORD's will to crush him and cause him to suffer...and the will of God will prosper in his hand (Isaiah 53:4,10, NIV).

In Peter's first sermon in Acts 2:22-23, he said, *"Men of Israel, hear these words: Jesus of Nazareth, a man attested to you by God with mighty words and wonders and signs that God did through him in your midst, as you yourselves know – this Jesus, delivered up according to the definite plan and foreknowledge of God, you crucified and killed by the hands of lawless men.*

As I mentioned at the end of the last chapter, Peter said Herod, Pilate, the Romans, and the people of Israel had conspired against Jesus, whom God had anointed. Then he said in prayer to God, *"They did what your power and will had decided beforehand should happen* (Acts 4:27-29, NIV).

God very carefully revealed in the Old Testament Scriptures what his power and will had decided beforehand should happen.

So, did Jesus' death fulfill these prophecies?

Chapter 7

What about the Prophecies?

In Matthew 26:24, Jesus said, *"The Son of Man will go just as it is written about him."*

When the soldiers went to arrest Jesus, he told them, *"Do you think that I cannot appeal to my Father, and he will at once send me more than twelve legions of angels? But how then should the Scriptures be fulfilled, that it must be so?"* (Matthew 26:53-54).

At the same time, he said, *"Have you come out as against a robber, with swords and clubs to capture me? Day after day I sat in the temple teaching, and you did not seize me. But all this has taken place that the Scriptures of the prophets might be fulfilled"* (Matthew 26:53-56).

We know that there are also many prophecies in the Old Testament about Jesus' birth and ministry, but today we are going to look at those prophecies that were fulfilled on the day that Jesus died.

He would be betrayed

Zechariah 11:12-13 even shows the amount of money that would be paid, and what they would do with it. The fulfillment of this prophecy is in Matthew 27:1-10.

He would be silent

He was oppressed, and he was afflicted, yet he opened not his mouth; like a lamb that is led to the slaughter, and like a sheep that before its shearers is silent, so he opened not his mouth (Isaiah 53:7).

This prophecy was fulfilled in Matthew 27:12-14:

But when he was accused by the chief priests and elders, he gave no answer. Then Pilate said to him, "Do you not hear how many things they testify against you?" But he gave him no answer, not even to a single charge, so that the governor was greatly amazed.

There would be no crime

Old Testament*: ...he had done no violence, and there was no deceit in his mouth* (Isaiah 53:9b).

New Testament: Remember how many times Pilate said that he had found no fault with Jesus?

He would be despised, rejected, mocked, insulted

OT: *He was despised and rejected by men; a man of sorrows, and acquainted with grief, and as one from whom men hide their faces he was despised, and we esteemed him not* (Isaiah 53:3).

"But I am a worm and not a man, scorned by men

*and despised by the people. All who see me mock
me, they hurl insults, shaking their heads..."*
(Psalm 22:6-7).

NT: *Then the soldiers of the governor took Jesus
into the governor's headquarters, and they
gathered the whole battalion before him. And they
stripped him and put a scarlet robe one him, and
twisting together a crown of thorns, they put it on
his head and put a reed in his right hand. And
kneeling before him, they mocked him, saying,
"Hail, King of the Jews!" And they spit on him and
took the reed and struck him on the head. And
when they had mocked him, they stripped him of
the robe and put his own clothes on him and led
him away to crucify him* (Matthew 27:27-31).

"He trusts in God. Let God rescue him"

OT: *All who seek me mock me, they hurl insults,
shaking their heads; "He trusts in the LORD; let
the LORD rescue him. Let him deliver him, since he
delights in him"* (Psalm 22:7-8, NIV).

NT: *So also the chief priests, with the scribes and
elders mocked him, saying, "He saved others; he*

cannot save himself. He is the King of Israel; let him come down now from the cross, and we will believe in him. He trusts in God' let God deliver him now, if he desires him. For he said, 'I am the Son of God'" (Matthew 27:41-44).

The two robbers

OT: *Therefore I will divide him a portion with the many, and he shall divide the spoil with the strong, because he poured out his soul to death and was numbered with the transgressors* (Psalm 22:7-8).

NT: *Then two robbers were crucified with him, one on the right and one on the left* (Matthew 27:38).

They would divide up his clothes

OT: *...they divide my garments among them, and for my clothing they cast lots* (Psalm 22:18).

NT: *And when they had crucified him, they divided his garments among them by casting lots* (Matthew 27:35).

When the soldiers had crucified Jesus, they took his garments and divided them into four parts, one part for each soldier; also his tunic. But the tunic was seamless, woven in one piece from top to bottom, so they said to one another, "let us not tear it, but cast lots for it to see whose it shall be. This was to fulfill the Scripture which says, "They divided my garments among them, and for my clothing they cast lots." So the soldiers did these things... (John 19:23-24)

He would make intercession for the transgressors

OT: *For he bore the sin of many, and made intercession for the transgressors* (Isaiah 53:12b, NIV).

NT: And *when they came to the place that is called The Skull, there they crucified him, and the criminals, one on his right, and one on his left. And Jesus said, "Father, forgive them, for they know not what they do"* (Luke 23:33-34).

"My God, my God"

OT: *My God, my God, why have you forsaken me? Why are you so far from saving me, from the words of my groaning?* (Psalm 22:1).

NT: *And about the ninth hour Jesus cried out with a loud voice, saying, "Eli, Eli, lema sabachthani?" that is, "My God, my God, why have you forsaken me?* (Matthew 27:46).

"I thirst"

OT: *My strength is dried up like a potsherd, and my tongue sticks to the roof of my mouth...* (Psalm 22:15, NIV)

NT: *After this, Jesus, knowing that all was now finished, said (to fulfill the Scripture), "I thirst"* (John 19:28).

He would be pierced

OT: *But he was pierced for our transgressions...* (Isaiah 53:5a).

For dogs encompass me; a company of evildoers encircles me; they have pierced my hands and feet... (Psalm 22:16).

NT: As was mentioned before, it wasn't until the Romans came into power that crucifixion was used as a means for killing criminals, and the Romans were in power when Jesus was on earth.

No bones would be broken

OT: *I can count all my bones... I am poured out like water, and all my bones are out of joint* (Psalm 22:17a, 14a). This last, of course, would be another natural consequence of being crucified.

NT: *Since it was the day of Preparation, and so that the bodies would not remain on the cross on the Sabbath (for the Sabbath was a high day), the Jews asked Pilate that their legs might be broken and that they might be taken away. so the soldiers came and broke the legs of the first, and of the other who had been crucified with him. But when they came to Jesus and saw that he was already dead, they did not break his legs. But one of the soldiers pierced his side with a spear, and at once there came out blood and water. He who saw it has borne witness – his testimony is true, and he knows that he is telling the truth – that you also may believe. For these things took place that the Scripture might be fulfilled: "Not one of his bones will be broken." And again another Scripture says, "They will look on him whom they have pierced"* (John 19:31-37).

"It is finished"

OT: *Posterity will serve him; future generations will be told about the Lord. They will proclaim his righteousness to a people yet unborn – for he has done it* (Psalm 22:30-31, NIV). I am not a student of Hebrew, but I have been told that this last phrase (for he has done it) could be translated "for it is finished".

NT: *When Jesus had received the sour wine, he*

said, "It is finished, and he bowed his head and gave up his spirit (John 19:30).

He would be assigned a grave with the wicked...

OT: *And they made his grave with the wicked and with a rich man in his death...* (Isaiah 53:9a).

NT: *Then two robbers were crucified with him, one on the right and one on the left* (Matthew 27:38).

...and with a rich man in his death

OT: (See above OT verse).

NT: *When it was evening, there came a rich man from Arimathea, named Joseph, who also was a disciple of Jesus. He went to Pilate and asked for the body of Jesus. Then Pilate ordered it to be given to him. And Joseph took the body and wrapped it in a clean linen shroud and laid it in his own new tomb, which he had cut in the rock* (Matthew 27:57-60a).

He would rise again

OT: "...though the LORD makes his life a guilt offering, *he will see his offspring and prolong his days, and the will of the LORD will prosper in his hand. After the suffering of his soul, he will see the light of life and be satisfied* (Isaiah 53:10b-11a, NIV).

NT: *But on the first day of the week, at early dawn, they went to the tomb, taking the spices they had prepared. And they found the stone rolled away from the tomb, but when they went in, they did not find the body of the Lord Jesus. While they were perplexed about this, behold, two men stood by them in dazzling apparel. And as they were frightened and bowed their faces to the ground, the men said to them, "Why do you seek the living among the dead? He is not here, but has risen! Remember how he told you, while he was still in Galilee, that the Son of Man must be delivered into the hands of sinful men and be crucified and on the third day rise. And they remembered his words* (Luke 24:1-8).

Jesus said that the Scripture had been fulfilled

When Jesus met two men on the road to Emmaus, they didn't recognize him at first. The men were talking about the resurrection. Jesus said to them, *"How foolish you are, and how slow of heart to believe all that the prophets have spoken! Did not the Christ have to suffer these things and then enter his glory?" And beginning with Moses and all the Prophets, he explained to them what was said in all the Scriptures concerning himself* (Luke 24:25-27, NIV).

Later, when Jesus appeared to the disciples, he said to them, *"This is what I told you while I was still with you: Everything must be fulfilled that is written about me in the Law of Moses, the Prophets and the Psalms." Then he opened their minds so they could understand the Scriptures. He told them, "This is what is written: The Christ will suffer and rise from the dead on the third day, and repentance and forgiveness of sins will be preached in his name to all nations, beginning at Jerusalem. You are witnesses of these things* (Luke 24:44-48, NIV).

I recently read a fascinating book called *The Case for Christ* by Lee Strobel. He was a journalist who investigated crimes for the *Chicago Tribune*. When his wife became a Christian in the true sense of the word, it changed her life. Strobel said, "I was pleasantly surprised – even fascinated – by the fundamental changes in her character, her integrity, and her personal confidence. Eventually I wanted to get to the bottom of what was prompting these subtle but significant shifts in my wife's attitudes, so I launched an all-out investigation into the facts surrounding the case for Christianity."[2]

He spared no effort or expense in order to interview experts who could tell him about the documentary, corroborating, and scientific evidence. Lee went armed with all the questions that skeptics bring up about Christianity. One of those questions was, "Did Jesus – and Jesus alone – match the identity of the Messiah?"

He had been told that in the Old Testament Scriptures there were dozens of important prophesies about the Messiah who would be sent by God to redeem his people. These predictions, in effect, made up a figurative "fingerprint" that only the Chosen One would have. In this way, the Jewish people would be able to recognize an imposter and validate the credentials of the authentic Messiah.

In order to get reliable information about the subject, Strobel interviewed Louis S. Lapides, a Jewish man who had studied for himself the Old Testament and, because of his research, become convinced that Jesus was the Messiah that God had promised his people.

When Lapides initially decided to look at the descriptions of the Messiah, he came to an abrupt halt in the fifty-third chapter of Isaiah, where there is a crystal clear picture of how Messiah would suffer and die for the sins of the world – all written over seven hundred years before Jesus walked on earth.

One by one, Lapides discovered more than four-dozen important predictions that came to pass in the life of Jesus. Strobel asked him if there could be any chance that Jesus had fulfilled these prophecies merely by coincidence (or, for that matter, on purpose). "Not a chance" was his answer, and he added that the chances were so astronomical that they excluded any possibility. Some expert did the math and computed that the possibility of one person fulfilling all 48 Old Testament prophecies was "one chance in a trillion, trillion, trillion, trillion, trillion, trillion, trillion, trillion, trillion, trillion, trillion, trillion, trillion".[3]

Jesus' words in Luke's gospel have been proven true, *"This is what I told you while I was still with you: Everything must be fulfilled that is written about me in the Law of Moses, the Prophets, and the Psalms"* (Luke 24:44).

It was fulfilled – in Jesus – the only one in history who had the fingerprint (or DNA) of the Chosen One.

Chapter 8

Did Jesus know that he was going to die?

I found at least fifteen times, just in the gospel of Matthew, that Jesus told his disciples, or his audience, that he was going to die.

He knew who

Jesus knew who wanted him dead.

Soon after Peter confessed that Jesus was the Christ, the Son of the living God, we read: *From that time on Jesus began to explain to his disciples that he must go to Jerusalem and suffer many things at the hands of the elders, chief priests and teachers of the law, and that he must be killed and on the third day be raised to life.* (Notice the two uses of the word "must" – author's note). *Peter took him aside and began to rebuke him, "Never, Lord!" he said. "This shall never happen to you!" Jesus turned to Peter, "Get behind, Satan! You are a stumbling block to me, you do not have in mind the things of God, but the things of men"* (Matthew 16:21-23, NIV).

Four chapters later, in Matthew 20:17-19, Jesus took his disciples aside and told them *"...the Son of Man will be delivered over to the chief priests and scribes, and they will condemn him to death and deliver him over to the Gentiles to be mocked and flogged and crucified..."*

He knew where

The first part of the above passage from Matthew 20 tells us that Jesus said to his disciples, *"See, we are going up to Jerusalem. And the Son of Man will be delivered to the chief priests and scribes, and they will condemn him to death..."*

When Thomas, the doubting disciple, heard that Jesus was heading for Jerusalem, he said to the rest of the disciples, *"Let us also go, that we may die with him"* (John 11:16). I would have liked to hear Thomas' tone of voice when he said that. I doubt that he really wanted to die with Jesus.

He knew when

When Jesus had finished all these sayings, he said to his disciples, "You know that after two days the Passover is coming, and the Son of Man will be delivered up to be crucified" (Matthew 26:1-2).

There was real significance in the fact that Jesus was crucified during Passover, the time when the Jews celebrated their release from Egyptian bondage. The angel of death passed over that night and only the homes that were protected by the blood of a perfect lamb were saved. When Jesus began his ministry, John the Baptist introduced him as *the Lamb of God who takes away the sin of the world* (John 1:29).

He knew what

Jesus knew that he would be betrayed: As they were gathering in Galilee, Jesus said to them, *"The Son of Man is going to be betrayed into the hands of men"* (Matthew 17:22, NIV). And, of course, at the Last Supper the betrayer was pointed out.

He knew that he would suffer: ... *Jesus began to show his disciples that he must go to Jerusalem and suffer many things...* (Matthew 16:21)

He also knew that his disciples would fall away: *Then Jesus said to them, "You will all fall away because of me this night. For it is written, 'I will strike the shepherd, and the sheep of the flock will be scattered"* (Matthew 26:31-32).

He knew that he would be buried: *"For just as Jonah was three days and three nights in the belly of the great fish, so will the Son of Man be three days and three nights in the heart of the earth"* (Matthew 12:40).

When Mary anointed Jesus with expensive perfume and Judas complained about the cost, Jesus told him, *"Leave her alone, so that she may keep it for the day of my burial. For the poor you always have with you, but you do not always have me* (John 12:7-8).

And he knew, of course, that he would rise again: As they were coming down the mountain (after Jesus' glorification before Peter, James, and John), he instructed them, *"Tell no one the vision, until the Son of Man is raised from the dead"* (Matthew 17:9).

He knew how

"And I, when I am lifted up from the earth, will draw all people to myself." He said this to show by what kind of death he was going to die (John 12:32-33).

After Jesus told his disciples that he would be betrayed, condemned to death, and turned over to the Gentiles, he said that he would be *"mocked and flogged and crucified"* (Matthew 20:18-19).

He knew why

Jesus told his disciples *"...whoever would be great among you must be your servant...even as the Son of Man came not to be served but to serve, and to give his life as a ransom for many"* (Matthew 20:28, NIV).

At the Last Supper: *Now as they were eating, Jesus took bread, and after blessing it broke it and gave it to his disciples, and said, "Take, eat; this is my body." And he took the cup, and when he had given thanks he gave it to them, saying, "Drink of it, all of you, for this is my blood of the covenant, which is poured out for many for the forgiveness of sins"* (Matthew 26:26-28).

Chapter 9

Did Jesus want to die?

One might think that Jesus had reservations about dying when he asked his Father, *"...if it be possible, let this cup pass from me..."* (Matthew 26:39). We also remember those words of anguish while he was on the cross, *"My God, my God, why have you forsaken me?"* (Mark 15:34).

We must realize that, while Jesus was one hundred percent God, he was also one hundred percent man, and, as a man, suffered pain just as we do and probably also dreaded pain as much as we do. And, of course, the greatest pain that he would experience was when his Father would turn his back on him because of the sin he was carrying.

Jesus said, *"Now my soul is troubled. And what shall I say? ' Father, save me from this hour'? But for this purpose I have come to this hour. Father, glorify your name."* Then a voice came from heaven, *"I have glorified it, and I will glorify it again"* (John 12:27-28).

In the tenth chapter of John, Jesus repeated at least five times in seven verses that, as the good shepherd, he was going to lay down his life for the sheep. Jesus said, *"The thief comes only to steal and kill and destroy. I have come that they may have life, and have it to the full. I am the good shepherd. The good shepherd lays down his life for the shepherd. The reason my Father loves me is that I lay down my life – only to take it up again. No one takes it from me, but I lay it down of my own accord. I have authority to lay it down ad authority to take it up again. This command I received from my Father* (John 10:10-11, 17-18, NIV).

He told his disciples, *"...the world must learn that I love the Father and that I do exactly what my Father has commanded me"* (John 14:30-31, NIV).

In John 15:13 he said, *"Greater love has no one than this, that he lay down his life for his friends."*

Now before the Feast of the Passover, when Jesus knew that his hour had come to depart out of this world to the Father, having loved his own who were in the world, he loved them to the end (John 13:1-2).

Yes, Jesus wanted to go to the cross, even though it meant going through all the agony. He did it because he loves his Father and because he loves you.

Chapter 10

Why did he have to die?

When we carefully examine the Old Testament prophecies and the New Testament accounts, we have no choice but to come to the conclusion that every piece of the puzzle of Jesus' death was put in place before the foundation of the world. But the question remains, why did he have to die?

He died because we could not save ourselves

We are all sinners and, because of that sin, separated from a God who is holy, holy, holy. His Word says: *"None is righteous, no, not one; no one understands; no one seeks for God. All have turned aside; together they have become worthless; no one does good, not even one"* (Romans 3:10-11).

... for all have sinned and fall short of the glory of God... (Romans 3:23)

For while we were still weak, at the right time Christ died for the ungodly. For one will scarcely die for a righteous person – though perhaps for a good person one would dare even to die – but God shows his love for us in that while we were still sinners, Christ died for us (Romans 5:8).

He died because he was the only sacrifice that God would accept

Way back in the Old Testament, God established that the sacrifices for sin had to be without defect. When John the Baptist introduced Jesus as "the Lamb of God, who takes away the sin of the world," he was presenting God's perfect, sinless sacrifice.

In his first epistle, Peter tells us: *For you know that it was not with perishable things such as silver or gold that you were redeemed from the empty way of life handed down to you from your forefathers, but with the precious blood of Christ, a lamb without blemish or defect. He was chosen before the creation of the world, but was revealed in these last times for our sake* (1:18-20, NIV).

Christ said, *"Here I am – it is written about me I the scroll – I have come to do your will O God." And by that will, we have been made holy, through the sacrifice of the body of Jesus Christ once for all* (Hebrews 10:7, 10, NIV).

He himself bore our sins in his body on the tree, so that we might die to sins and live for righteousness; by his wounds you have been healed (1 Peter 2:24, NIV).

God made him who had no sin to be sin for us, so that in him we might become the righteousness of God (2 Corinthians 5:21).

The Old Testament had already revealed hundreds of years before Jesus' birth that things would happen this way. Read what Isaiah prophesied:

"Surely he has borne our griefs and carried our sorrows... But he was pierced for our

transgressions; he was crushed for our iniquities; upon him was the chastisement that brought us peace, and with his wounds we are healed. All we like sheep have gone astray; we have turned – every one – to his own way; and the LORD has laid on him the iniquity of us all. After the anguish of his soul, he will see and be satisfied; by his knowledge shall the righteous one, my servant, make many to be accounted righteous, and he shall bear their iniquities (53:4a, 5-6, 11).

Christ suffered the wrath of God in our place.

He died so that we could be forgiven

He has delivered us from the dominion of darkness and transferred us to the kingdom of his beloved Son, in whom we have redemption, the forgiveness of sins (Colossians 1:13-14).

In him we have redemption through his blood, the forgiveness of our trespasses, according to the riches of God's grace, which he lavished on us, in all wisdom and insight (Ephesians 1:7-8).

He died so that we could live with God eternally

God ...saved us...not because of our works but because of his own purpose and grace, which he gave us in Christ Jesus before the ages began, and which now has been manifested through the appearing of our Savior Christ Jesus, who abolished death and brought life and immortality to light through the gospel (2 Timothy 1:9-10).

For God so loved the world that he gave his only Son, that whoever believes in him should not perish but have eternal life. For God did not send his Son into the world to condemn the world, but in order that the world might be saved through him. Whoever believes in him is not condemned, but whoever does not believe is condemned already, because he has not believed in the name of the only Son of God (John 3:16-18).

After raising Lazarus from the dead, Jesus said, *"I am the resurrection and the life. Whoever believes in me, though he die, yet shall he live, and everyone who lives and believes in me shall never die. Do you believe this?* (John 11:25)

Jesus said: *"Let not your hearts be troubled. Believe in God; believe also in me. In my Father's house are many rooms. If it were not so, would I have told you that I go to prepare a place for you? And if I go and prepare a place for you, I will come again and will take you to myself, that where I am you may be also. I am the way, and the truth, and the life. No one comes to the Father except through me* (John 14:1-3, 6).

I live in Brazil, where a good share of the population will say that they believe in God. Many would probably also say that they believe Jesus is God's Son and that he died on the cross for our sin. However, when I ask, "Do you know that you have eternal life?" many have no answer.

My favorite verses for these people are found in 1 John 5:11-13: *And this is the testimony, that God gave us eternal life, and this life is in his Son. Whoever has the Son has life; whoever does not have the Son of God does not have life. I write these things to you who believe in the name of the Son of God that you may **know** that you have eternal life (emphasis mine).*

He died so that we might know that the God who created us is a God of grace

And you were dead in the trespasses and sins in which you once walked, following the course of this world, following the prince of the power of the air, the spirit that is now at work in the sons of disobedience – among whom we all once lived in the passions of our flesh carrying out the desires of the body and the mind, and were by nature children of wrath, like the rest of mankind. But God, being rich in mercy, because of the great love with which he loved us, even when we were dead in trespasses, made us alive together with Christ – by grace you have been saved – and raised us up with him and seated us with him in the heavenly places in Christ Jesus, so that in the coming ages he might show the immeasurable riches of his grace in kindness to us in Christ Jesus. For by grace you have been saved through faith. And this is not of your own doing; it is the gift of God, not a result of works, so that no one may boast (Ephesians 2:1-8).

91

What do you do with a gift?

How would you feel if you gave someone a gift and they threw it on the floor and stomped on it? Some people do that with God's gift.

How would you feel if the person didn't open your gift, but left it on the shelf and just looked at the wrappings once a year (at Christmas)?

How would you feel if they told you, "Thanks, but I have no use for it"? In this case, everyone has a need for God's gift in Christ, because we are all sinners and condemned to die because of our sin.

How would you feel if they put their hand in their pocket and offered to pay for the gift? You would probably respond by saying, "But the price has already been paid! I want to GIVE it to you! You don't have to pay for it!"

How do you want the person to react? You would hope that they would accept your gift, appreciate it, and appropriate it.

And that's what God wants you to do with his gift. It isn't yours until you accept it and take advantage of it.

Chapter 11

Who killed Jesus?

It was a Sunday morning and I was in a strange town, at a different church. A lady got up to sing. She had a very pleasant voice, though not a professional or trained one, and she sang with great feeling.

The song was called, *"Who Killed Jesus?"* and as she went through the various verses, she considered many of the possibilities that I have mentioned. I don't remember all the words, because it has been over forty years since I heard her sing it. I had never heard the song before, nor have I heard it since. However, even after four decades, I can still remember the very first and the very last words of the song. By the time she had finished singing, we were all holding our breath.

Who killed Jesus many years ago?

Who was guilty of this crime so low?

Why did he have to die?

What is the reason why?

Who killed Jesus?

Now it's plain to see

That it was really ... me.[4]

The famous British preacher, Charles Spurgeon wrote:

MY SINS were the scourges which lacerated those blessed shoulders, and crowned that bleeding brow with thorns!
My sins cried, "Crucify Him! Crucify Him!" and laid the cross upon His gracious shoulders!

His being led forth to die is sorrow enough for one eternity, but MY having been His murderer is more, infinitely more grief, than one poor fountain of tears can express![5]

You may be remembering that at the beginning of this book I promised that the answer to the question, Who Killed Jesus? could bring peace and relief to the hearts of all who read it. So now you must be wondering why I have laden you down with guilt.

We all have to accept our portion of guilt in the death of Jesus before we can experience the relief and release that comes when God completely forgives us of that guilt (and the guilt of ALL our sin). He is able and willing to do this ONLY because of Jesus' sacrifice on the cross in our place. Besides being delivered from guilt, we are also delivered from the fear of death. We are at peace because we recognize that Jesus intercedes for us and has sent us his Holy Spirit, the Comforter.

Charles R. Swindoll in his book *The Grace Awakening* has a powerful illustration that brings this message home:

Let's imagine you have a six-year-old son whom you dearly love. Tragically, one day you discover that your son was horribly murdered. After a lengthy search the investigators of the crime find the killer. You have a choice. If you used every means in your power to kill the murderer for his crime, that would be vengeance. If, however, you're content to sit back and let the legal authorities take over and execute on him what is proper – a fair trial, a plea of guilty, capital punishment – that is justice. But if you should plead for the pardon of the murderer, forgive him completely, invite him into your home, and adopt him as your own son, that is grace.

Now you see why grace is so hard to grasp and to accept? Very few people (if any) who are reading this page right now would happily and readily do that. But God does it every day. He takes the guilty, believing sinner who says, "I am lost, unworthy, guilty as charged, and undeserving of forgiveness," and extends the gift of eternal life because Christ's death on the cross satisfied His demands against sin, namely, death. And God sees the guilty sinner (who comes by faith alone) as righteous as His own

Son. In fact, He even invites us to come home with Him as He adopts us into His forever family. Instead of treating us with vengeance or executing justice, God extends grace.[6]

Chapter 12

Is he dead?

I find it interesting that some Christians spend so much time concentrating on the death of Christ and so little thinking about his resurrection. Many don't even give it much thought on Easter because they are so busy taking advantage of the long holiday weekend.

Did you know that the reason why most churches meet on Sunday, rather than on the Sabbath as they did in the Old Testament, is because Jesus rose from the dead on the first day of the week? We Christians are to celebrate his resurrection every Sunday (or, even better, every day).

Early in the morning, on the first day of the week, Mary Magdalene and another Mary went to see the tomb where Jesus' body had been laid. *And, behold there was a violent earthquake, for an angel of the Lord descended from heaven and came and rolled back the stone and sat on it. His appearance was like lightning and his clothing white as snow* (Matthew 28:2-3).

You can imagine how they reacted to such a sight! We are told that the guards who were keeping watch were so frightened that they *trembled and became like dead men*. However, the angel told the women, *"Don't be afraid, for I know you seek Jesus who was crucified. He is not here, for he has risen, as he said."*

After showing them the place in the tomb where Christ's body had been, the angel told the women to go quickly and tell his disciples that he had risen from the dead and was going before them to Galilee. They would be able to see him there. You can read the whole story in Matthew 28:1-10.

Who saw Jesus after his resurrection?

Mary Magdalene and the other Mary – Matthew 28:8-10

Peter – Luke 24:34

The two men on the road to Emmaus – Luke 24:13-32

Jesus' disciples with the exception of Thomas – John 20:19-20

The disciples with Thomas – John 20:24-29

Seven of the disciples at the Sea of Galilee – John 21:1-24

The apostles, James, and more than 500 people, many of whom were still alive to talk about it when Paul wrote his first epistle to the Corinthians (15:6-7)

All who were present when Jesus ascended to heaven – Acts 1:1-11

Why is the resurrection so vital to the Christian faith?

The Apostle Paul very carefully explains why in 1 Corinthians 15:12-19. He says that if Jesus had not risen to life again:

Our preaching would be useless

Our faith would be futile

All Christians would be false witnesses

Our loved ones who died in Christ would be forever lost

We would still be in our sin

Christians deserve more pity than anyone else

Did people in Jesus' time believe that he had risen from the dead?

Peter told one of his audiences, *...you killed the Author of life, whom God raised from the dead. To this we are witnesses* (Acts 3:15).

Doctor Luke wrote in his introduction to the book

of Acts: *In my former book, Theophilus, I wrote about all that Jesus began to do and to teach until the day he was taken up to heaven, after giving instructions through the Holy Spirit to the apostles he had chosen. After his suffering, he showed himself to these men and gave many convincing proofs that he was alive. He appeared to them over a period of forty days and spoke about the kingdom* (verses 1-4).

Paul also affirmed in Acts 13:29-31: *And when they had carried out all that was written of him, they took him down from the tree and laid him in a tomb. But God raised him from the dead, and for many days he appeared to those who had come up with him from Galilee to Jerusalem, who are now his witnesses to the people* (Acts 13:29-31).

What evidence do we have that Jesus is alive?

• The empty tomb: If the disciples had stolen the body, why would they have been willing to give their lives for a lie? If, on the other hand, the Jewish leaders had stolen the body, why didn't they just produce it and show it to everyone in order to do away with the rumors of Christ's resurrection?

- The sealed tomb: Who broke the seal under penalty of death? Who rolled the heavy stone away and how did they manage to do it without the posted guards seeing it?

- The physical evidence: Jesus showed his disciples the nail prints in his hands and feet and the place where his side had been pierced with the sword.

- Transformed lives: Were the disciples expecting Jesus to rise again? Should they have? What could have been responsible for the radical change in the lives of those men? The same fearful souls who denied and abandoned their Lord were transformed into fearless witnesses who turned the world upside down with their preaching.

- Jesus' words: He told them many times that he would rise up from the grave and without his resurrection his death would be meaningless.

• God's words: He had prophesied in the Old Testament that Messiah would die and live again (see Psalms 16, 22, and Isaiah 53).

• Not the least of the evidences for Christ's resurrection is the transformation that took place in the lives of some of his enemies. How do you explain what happened in Paul's life? His only goal in life had been to persecute Christians, but after his encounter with the risen Christ, he became the principal witness to his death and resurrection – not only during his lifetime, but up to this present day through his writings. Another example is James, one of Jesus' brothers. We know that his brothers didn't even believe in him before the resurrection. Afterwards, however, James became the leader of the Jerusalem church.

How would these evidences hold up under scrutiny in a court of law?

Josh McDowell in his fascinating book, *More Than a Carpenter*, lists the results of the research of three highly respected lawyers:[7]

Professor Thomas Arnold was the headmaster of Rugby for fourteen years, author of a three-volume History of Rome, and appointed to the chair of modern history at Oxford. For many years he had studied the histories of other times, examined them, and weighed the evidence of those who had written about them. He said, "I know of no one fact in the history of mankind which is proved by better and fuller evidence of every sort, to the understanding of a fair inquirer, than the great sign which God has given us that Christ died and rose again from the dead."[8]

Dr. Simon Greenleaf was a famous Royal Professor of Law at Harvard University. He was also the Dane Professor of Law at the same university. While teaching there, Greenleaf wrote a volume in which he examined the legal value of the apostles' testimony to the resurrection of Christ. He concluded that the resurrection of Christ was one of the best supported events in history, according to the laws of legal evidence administered in courts of justice.[9]

Frank Morrison, another lawyer, thought that the story of the resurrection was a myth, although he planned to write a book about the last days of Jesus. However, upon looking at the facts with his legal background and training, he changed his mind and eventually wrote a best-seller called *Who Moved the Stone?* The first chapter was titled, "The Book That Refused to Be Written" and the rest of the book deals with the evidence for Christ's resurrection.[10]

Jesus said: *Because I live, you also will live. I am the resurrection and the life. Whoever believes in me, though he die, yet shall he live, and everyone who lives and believes in me shall never die. Do you believe this?* (John 14:19b, 11:25).

What about you? Do you believe this?

NOTES

1. C.S. Lewis, *Mere Christianity* (New York: The MacMillan Company, 1960), 40.

2. Lee Strobel, *The Case for Christ* (Grand Rapids, MI: Zondervan, 1998), 14.

3. Strobel, 183.

4. Mickey Holliday, *"Who Killed Jesus? I Would Like to Know"*, Copyright 1970, New Spring (Admin. By Brentwood-Benson Music Publishing, Inc.)

5. Charles Spurgeon, *Morning and Evening* (Memphis, TN: Bottom of the Hill Publishing, 2012), 204.

6. Charles Swindoll, *The Grace Awakening* (Dallas, TX: Word Publishing, 1990), 42-43.

7. Josh McDowell, *More Than a Carpenter* (Wheaton, Illinois: Tyndale House Publishers), 96-99.

8. Thomas Arnold, *Christian Life – Its Hopes, Its Fears, and Its Close, 6th edition* (London: T. Fellowes, 1859), 324.

9. Simon Greenleaf, *An Examination of the Testimony of the Four Evangelists by the Rules of Evidence in the Courts of Justice*

(Grand Rapids, MI: Baker Book House, 1965). Reprint of 1874 edition (New York: J. Crokroft and Co., 1974), 29.

10. Frank Morrison, *Who Moved the Stone?* (London: Faber and Faber, 1930).

Made in the USA
Charleston, SC
04 April 2015